Types of Maps

by
Jennifer M. Besel

Consulting editor:
Gail Saunders-Smith, PhD

Consultant:
Dr. Sarah E. Battersby
Department of Geography
University of South Carolina

CAPSTONE PRESS
a capstone imprint

Pebble Books are published by Capstone Press,
1710 Roe Crest Drive, North Mankato, Minnesota 56003
www.capstonepub.com

Library of Congress Cataloging-in-Publication Data
Besel, Jennifer M.
Types of maps / by Jennifer M. Besel.
pages cm—(Pebble Books. Maps)
Includes bibliographical references and index.
Summary: "Simple text with full-color photos and illustrations provide basic
information about types of maps"—Provided by publisher.
ISBN 978-1-4765-3124-3 (library binding)—ISBN 978-1-4765-3513-5 (ebook pdf)—
ISBN 978-1-4765-3525-8 (paperback)
1. Maps—Juvenile literature. I. Title.
GA105.6.B4718 2014
526'.8—dc23   2012046453

Editorial Credits
Gene Bentdahl, designer; Kathy McColley, production specialist; Sarah Schuette,
photo stylist; Marcy Morin, scheduler

Photo Credits
Capstone: 7, 11, 15, 19; Capstone Studio: Karon Dubke, cover, 1, 5, 9, 13, 17, 21

Note to Parents and Teachers

The Maps set supports social studies standards related to people, places, and
environments. This book describes and illustrates types of maps. The images
support early readers in understanding the text. The repetition of words and phrases
helps early readers learn new words. This book also introduces early readers to
subject-specific vocabulary words, which are defined in the Glossary section. Early
readers may need assistance to read some words and to use the Table of Contents,
Glossary, Read More, Internet Sites, and Index sections of the book.

Table of Contents

Useful Tools

Maps are useful tools.

People use many kinds of maps.

Each kind has a special job.

Physical Maps

Physical maps show the bumps and lumps on the land. These maps give the locations of mountains, rivers, or lakes.

Topographic maps show low and high areas of land. Contour lines on the map show how the land rises and falls.

9

Political Maps

Political maps show borders between states or countries. They also show cities and towns.

The United States

Key
- ⌇ River
- ✷ Capital
- ● City
- ⟍ State Border

People use road maps to travel. Road maps show roads, cities, and lakes. They also mark spots people might like to stop.

13

City maps are road maps
of just one town.

Schools, libraries, and streets
are shown on these maps.

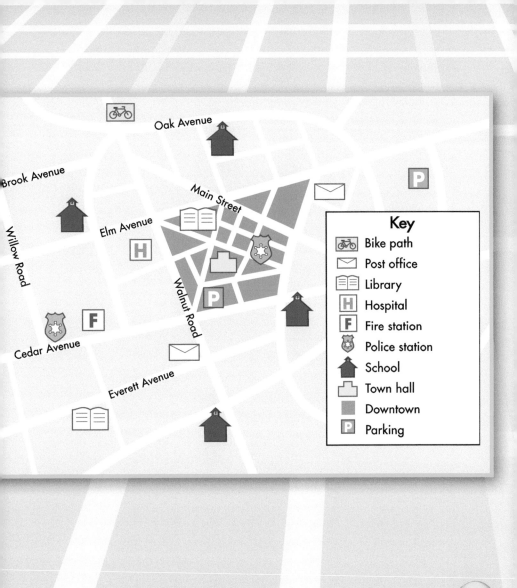

Oak Avenue

Brook Avenue

Willow Road

Main Street

Elm Avenue

Walnut Road

Cedar Avenue

Everett Avenue

Key
- 🚲 Bike path
- ✉ Post office
- 📖 Library
- Ⓗ Hospital
- Ⓕ Fire station
- 🛡 Police station
- 🏫 School
- Town hall
- ▦ Downtown
- 🅿 Parking

Other Maps

Globes are round, spinning maps. Globes are the only maps that show Earth as it looks from space.

Distribution maps show where certain things live or grow. Some show where the most people live.

U.S. Population Density

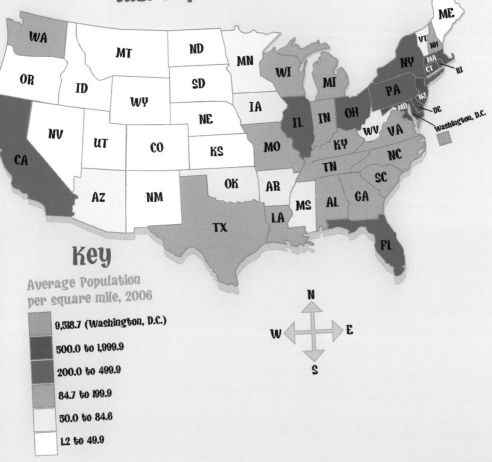

Key

Average Population per square mile, 2006

- 9,518.7 (Washington, D.C.)
- 500.0 to 1,999.9
- 200.0 to 499.9
- 84.7 to 199.9
- 50.0 to 84.6
- 1.2 to 49.9

Maps change over time. But one map feature never changes. Maps are always helpful tools.

Glossary

area—a part of a place

border—the dividing line between one state or country and another

contour line—a line on a topographic map that shows how the land rises and falls in certain places

distribution map—a map that shows where groups of things live or grow

location—the place or position of something

Read More

Besel, Jennifer M. *Map Scales.* Maps. North Mankato, Minn.: Capstone Press, 2014.

Greve, Meg. *Maps Are Flat, Globes Are Round.* Little World Geography. Vero Beach, Fla.: Rourke Pub., 2010.

Spilsbury, Louise. *Mapping.* Investigate. Chicago: Heinemann Library, 2010.

Internet Sites

FactHound offers a safe, fun way to find Internet sites related to this book. All of the sites on FactHound have been researched by our staff.

Here's all you do:

Visit *www.facthound.com*

Type in this code: 9781476531243

Critical Thinking Using the Common Core

1. For what reason would you use a political map instead of a physical map? (Craft and Structure)

2. Look at the map on page 19, and describe what a distribution map is. Why might you need a map that shows where the most people live? (Integration of Knowledge and Ideas)

3. Look online to find a political map of the United States from the year 1800. Compare that map to the map on page 11. Describe how and why the borders have changed. (Integration of Knowledge and Ideas)

Index

Word Count: 160
Grade: 1
Early-Intervention Level: 17